Take Three

AGNI is known for its strong commitment to publishing both established and upcoming writing talents. Founded by Askold Melnyczuk in 1972, AGNI has published poems, essays, and short fiction by American and international writers including Seamus Heaney, Margaret Atwood, Noam Chomsky, Yusef Komunyakaa, Derek Walcott, Susanna Kaysen, Robert Pinsky, and Sharon Olds. AGNI is dedicated to bringing voices together in a magazine Joyce Carol Oates says is "known for commitment not only to work of consistently high quality but to thematic subjects of crucial and lasting significance." *Take Three* is the first in an important annual series designed to launch the work of young poets chosen by AGNI's editorial board.

Take Three

AGNI New Poets Series: 1

GRAYWOLF PRESS

Publication of this volume is made possible in part by a grant provided
by the Minnesota State Arts Board through an appropriation by
the Minnesota State Legislature, and by a grant from the National
Endowment for the Arts. Significant additional support has been pro-
vided by the Andrew W. Mellon Foundation, the Lila Wallace-Reader's
Digest Fund, the McKnight Foundation, and other generous contribu-
tions from foundations, corporations, and individuals. Graywolf Press is
a member agency of United Arts, Saint Paul. To these organizations and
individuals who make our work possible, we offer heartfelt thanks.

Published by Graywolf Press
2402 University Avenue, Suite 203
Saint Paul, Minnesota 55114

Printed in the United States of America.

ISBN 1-55597-239-x

2 4 6 8 9 7 5 3 1
First Graywolf Printing, 1996

Library of Congress Catalog Card Number: 95-81003

Thomas Sayers Ellis

The Good Junk

THOMAS SAYERS ELLIS was born and raised in Washington, D.C., where he attended Paul Laurence Dunbar High School. He was educated at Harvard University and received an M.F.A. from Brown University in 1995. He is a cofounding member of The Dark Room Collective and The Dark Room Reading Series. His work has appeared in *A Gathering of the Tribes, AGNI, Black Bread, Boston Review, Callaloo, Graham House Review, Hambone, Harvard Review, In the Tradition: An Anthology of Young Black Writers*, the *Kenyon Review, lift, Ploughshares*, the *Southern Review*, and *UWEZO*. He has been a fellow at the MacDowell Colony and the Gell Writer's Center and in 1993 he coedited *On the Verge: Emerging Poets and Artists* (AGNI Press). Currently, he is a fellow at The Fine Arts Work Center in Provincetown, Massachusetts.

For Fin
Again & Again

Sticks

My father was an enormous man
Who believed kindness and lack of size
Were nothing more than sissified
Signs of weakness. Narrow-minded,

His eyes were the worst kind
Of jury—deliberate, distant, hard.
No one could outshout him
Or make bigger fists. The few

Who tried got taken for bad,
Beat down, their bodies slammed,
I wanted to be just like him:
Big man, man of the house, king.

A plagiarist, hitting the things he hit,
I learned to use my hands watching him
Use him, pretending to slap Mother
When he slapped Mother.

He was sick. A diabetic slept
Like a silent vowel inside his well-built,
Muscular, dark body. Hard as all that
With similar weaknesses,

I discovered writing,
How words are part of speech
With beats and breaths of their own.
Interjections like flams: wham! bam!

An heir to the rhythm
And tension beneath the beatings,
My first attempts were filled with noise,
Wild solos, violent uncontrollable blows.

The page tightened like a drum
Resisting the clockwise twisting
Of a handheld chrome key,
The noisy banging and tuning of growth.

A Baptist Beat

A mixed congregation: sinners, worshippers,
Hustlers, survivors. All that terrible energy,
Locked in, trying to blend. Such a gathering
Of tribes has little, if any, use for a silk-robed choir.
Members bring their own noise, own souls.
Any Avenue Crew will tell you: nothing comes closer
To salvation than this. Here, there is no talk of judgment,
No fear. Every now & then, an uninformed God
Will walk in, bear witness, mistake Kangol
For halo, all those names for unwanted bodies
Being called home, arms raised to testify, waving
From side to side, fists flying like bullets, bullets
Like fists. Above the snare: two sticks make the sign
Of the cross then break—a divorced crucifix.
The tambourine shakes like a collection plate.
This pastor wants to know who's in the house,
Where we're from, are we tired yet, ready to quit?
We run down front, scream & shout, "Hell no,
We ain't ready to go!" The organ hesitates,
Fills the house with grace, good news, resurrection
& parole, a gospel of chords rising like souls.
Up, up, up up, down, down. Up, up, up up,
Down. Up, up, up up, down, down.
Up, up, up up, down. The cowbell's religious beat,
A prayer angel-ushered through dangerous air.

Tambourine

For the Reverend Ida Ellis

One of God's noisemakers
And my favorite of her relics,
It was made of wood
With a small drumhead
And disks fitted into the rim.

Sundays, it took a sinner's beating,
Clung to her waist like a canteen,
Holy water for the journey,
Cleansing souls, washing down
Hard-to-swallow sins, ours.

Great-Grandmama preached
The Life across the street from us,
The light in her apartment
Somehow different from the light
In ours—something to do with

Faith, living alone, old Bibles,
Candles and crosses. Drawn in
By what I thought was money—
A sermon emptying pockets,
Turning them inside out:

Nickels, dimes & quarters—
I got caught with my ear pressed
To her door. When you
Play it, she said, Play it
With the ball of your palm.

Shake it with one hand,
Strike it with the other.

Faggot

We nicknamed Robert
Robin because he played
With girls and memorized cheers,
Preferred Home Economics to Shop.

In Gym, he switched like them
And could control his strength,
Hitting volleyballs with his wrist
To boys of his choice.

Like somebody's sister,
He rolled his eyes and fought
With his hands open, backing away,
Kicking & scratching, a windmill of self-defense.

For this we called him Punk,
Faggot, Sissy, whistling & kissing,
Whenever Miss Williams left the classroom
Or turned to write on the board.

In talent shows he sang "Baby Love"
Backed by girls we had crushes on,
Signifying he knew more about
The opposite sex than us.

He did. We were virgins.
Our big brothers protected him,
Saying we'd understand when
The fuzzy shadows under our arms

And between our legs
Turned to hair. When one
Of our rubber bands bruised his neck,
His father came to school and beat

The shit out of him,
Erasing our passion
Mark with marks
Of his own.

Barracuda*

Your memory of water
Is clouded by a crimson tide,
Sad bulging eyes,
A dive—head first
Into pages of chlorine.
The past evaporates
Into a silence that floats,
Corpselike, on its side.
At Dunbar, we did time
On our backs and the water,
Though friendlier,
Was less penetrable—
Like the sky, a master
Of reflected disguises.
There must be a word
For what you're doing.
Are you crying?
Damp days.
Solitudes crowded with loneliness.
Years swim before you.
Memory moves like sewage
Through the brain's plumbing.
With a cadaver of guilt
On your back,
You've done so many push-ups
The stripes on your chest
Are stronger than bars.
You're inside yourself,
Examining bubbles for answers.
Your body's a cell,
The cell's a tank.
Yet nothing, save time,
Passes through you.

* Refers to Anthony Jordan, former member of the Dunbar High
  School Barracudas swim team, now serving time for manslaughter.

Stayed Back

All the schools I attended
Were enormous, within walking distance
Of home, public. An A and B student,
I didn't start messing up until
My senior year. Cynthia Jones,

Who taught us Literature,
Warned me first: stop staying out
So late! But, that young, everything
Worth knowing had to be experienced
Firsthand, then learned.

In class, drunk on drums,
Too weary to perform, my mind
Was always somewhere else—
The Howard Theatre, Hains Point,
Chasing girls, listening to Go-Go.

Recess was precious, sometimes
Lasting all day like summer. We'd sit in
Victor Sparrow's Deuce & a Quarter
Blasting RARE ESSENCE, doors open,
Legs hanging—bent like broken wings,

Which is where Kenny Magee
Found me, outside Dunbar, perpetrating
And pretending I knew the timbales.
Ambition—no, a lie—cost me a year.
Also brought me closer to verse, here.

The Market

Our parents were thrilled when it reopened,
A place to buy fresh fruit, vegetables, and meat.
So nearby, our mothers practically rolled out of bed
Into the market then home into their kitchens or soaps.

Only God could save time, so we thanked Him—
Amen! But later for Him was casting a Plague on us,
The rats and roaches that plotted while we were asleep—
How to get their claws and sharp teeth on our meat.

Both chicken and beef told on themselves when our mothers
Baked or boiled them. Like lust, the scent of flesh cooking
Attracted more of the same greedy occupants we already had.
Nightly, their eyes bulged and watered in the darkness

And in the cracks and crevices between our refrigerator
And stove, cabinets, and wall. They laid eggs
We couldn't eat where they thought we couldn't see
Or reach them. Their families outgrew ours.

Our holidays became theirs. The courageous ones
Would chance their lives scurrying across the floor
While we ate—blinded by the crumbs that fell
From our mouths into theirs like snow.

Being There

Kennedy Playground
Washington, D.C.

We forced our faces
into the circular frame
a stringless hoop made,
hoping more than silence & light

would fall through.
We fought for position.
We fouled & shoved.
We high-fived God.

Our Converse All-Stars
burned enough rubber
to rival the devil and his mama.
Hoop, horseshoe, noose.

We aimed at a halo
hung at an angle we couldn't fit,
waiting for the camera
to record our unfocused

need to score.
We left earth.
We lost weight.
We disobeyed bone.

Our finger rolls
& reverse layups
were rejected by angels
guarding the rim,

same as prayers
returned to sinners.

Barbershop

Newspapers, magazines, mirrors,
The faces of slain leaders, athletes,
Hair spray, hair sheen, hair cream.

Fisted picks, combs, brushes,
Relaxer, hot towels, perm,
A soda machine, television, radio.

Greedy clippers, scissors, blades,
Soul patches, sideburns, mustaches,
Smooth necks, naked ears, prickly chins.

Shape it up, nothing off the top,
Take it all off, shave the sides, clean,
Skin it, real low, close, bald.

Razored line, straight across, part,
Unwrinkled, tight, grease, scalp,
Kinks, waves, curls, fades.

Cowbell

You're how we found The Maverick Room,
The Cave Yard, The Black Hole and block parties
In hard-to-find inner-city neighborhoods
With names like Congress Heights and Valley Green.

You're the Real McCoy,
What we used to teach timid beginners to hit back.
When the power went out you gathered kin,
A family discussion of percussion:

Tambourine, vibra-slap, ratchet.
We met reaching into the same pocket,
Agreed a crowded one is equivalent to sin.
Sticks can't harm the real you.

You're what gets heard,
A prayer above crowd noise and soul.
Down-to-earth, hardheaded, hollow, loud.
I know your weak spots. You know mine.

Shooting Back

You load, focus, aim.
The shutter falls like a tiny axe,
Reopens, a blinking eye washed in light.

An image enters the world
Premature, wet, lit like a miracle. The holier ones
Exploit darkness, develop like secrets.

Only the faithful possess
Nerve enough to stand this long, arms crossed,
Fearlessly posed, in the line of fire.

Every shot attempts to capture
The will-to-survive of its target:
High-top fades, hooded sweats, hard stares,

A Gucci background, a wicker chair.

The Break of Dawn

Explosive posters lit at night.
On every tree, a cardboard savior
Nailed to rooted echoes of wooden agony.

Sidewalks graffitied with chalk silhouettes,
Stank of murder, scabs of moonlight
Patch our wounded night.

Wrapped in bandaged blue, pale morning
Wakes the day. Mute doses
Of evaporating darkness on the breath of potholes.

Giant Steps

Sugar Bear is the Abominable Snowman of Go-Go,
Laying stone-cold sheets of bottom
Over forgotten junk farms and Indian deathbeds.

Years ago, a conspiracy to melt him
Was put to sleep by an unlimited freeze.

He bridged the gap between Southeast & Northwest,
Passing through Anacostia & Watergate,
Untouched, plucking veins and exposing hidden tapes.

Bear's melody is Big Foot Music;
2 places at the same time.

On atomic nights
His footprints can be viewed from heaven,
Extinguishing mushrooms.

Bear let the first fox loose on the moon.
Hear his cry: *ooh la la la!*

Take Me Out to the Go-Go

Nikita zips across stage
Trailed by a troop of white-gloved
One-wheelers: Killer Joes,
The 12 and Under Crew
In disguise.

A sixth sense guides him
Beyond darkness. An
Inner voice says when,
Don't stop, don't stop, don't stop,
I'll tell you when.

A constellation of funeral homes.
Jumpsuits. Red & white
Ribbons in the sky. The total
Groove, a carnival of roses
Circling the moon.

Mere call & response
Never knocked socks this way,
Lifting nicknames & dates
From the faces of tombstones
And mere call & response never will.

God climbs inside,
Asking for souls —
Something we weren't taught to share.

On Display

A ghost with PCP eyes
Bops through my memory.

Her skirt rises as she
Spins through love boat,

Lagerfeld & hot breath. *Up*
Against the wall standing

Very tall, he's got the big
Spotlight and he's doing it all.

We playact black ants surround-
ing a crumb, then go at her

Like a broken drumroll bang-
ing silence. Six, seven,

Nine, straight through her.
Turn off the house lights y'all,

Says JAS. FUNK, *So we can put*
Everybody on display.

Aw turn off the house lights
Y'all, so we can get everybody

On display. Aw get it!

The Roll Call

Any half-decent rapper
Can conjure the dead,

Can reach into graves
And accuse God

Of Indian giving.
The trick is ancestral,

No more magic than memory's
Hidden strings & chains.

Trust me,
We haven't forgotten a name.

Say them. Raise your hands.
Holler at me!

Tapes

We got them the hard way,
Taking turns holding recorders
Blessed with the weight of D batteries

On our shoulders.
We pressed PLAY & RECORD,
Ready to release PAUSE

The moment the drummer
Flexed visible muscle
Or the synthesizer whined

Like a siren.
Weren't we lucky
A few clubs had balconies.

I remember the red lights,
How when they danced
We looked up.

We made copies,
Refusing to trade the ones
With our names on them,

Came to blows
When one was lost, stolen.
"Make me a copy,"

Carmichael said the day
After his brother's murder.
A way of remembering,

Holding on.
Ranked next to gold chains
& school clothes,

Our love for them
Was southern—the older ones
Getting the most

Attention.
Care.
Respect.

Block Party

A permit is obtained
In advance, orange, fluorescent
Pylons placed in the middle
Of the street at both ends
Of the block. No thru traffic,
Nowhere to park.

Weather allowing,
Word spreads like
A sexually transmitted disease,
Streetwise, one big
Virus, bacon grease,
The epicenter of an itch.

Expect groove, good junk,
Chitlin buckets. The DJ is
Too old to be still
Living at home,
Every summer turning
His mama's front yard

Into a radio station,
A garden of plastic crates,
Wax irises, small reels
Of weeds, two turntables
And a microphone, head-
phones flipped forward

Like the face guard
On a football helmet,
Spin doctor, athlete, star.
Expect old folks, night
Owls perched on porches,
Peering out dark windows.

Expect youngins,
Ripping and running,
High on sugar, salt, sun.
Sodas, burgers, dogs. Bass booming,
Booming again, backing
Away like thunder.

A synthesized bomb
Parts the crowd. Roadies
In flare red jumpers
Work like hustlers,
Plugging things in,
Taking things out.

A sea of us wave
And go *ho,* pumping
Our fists like fists.
The street stretches like skin,
Curbs distant as shores,
Rival congregations, storms.

The Moonlite Inn

1

Our truck rolled out of an alley
In Petworth at 8—after dinner,
A bellyful of roadies & chrome.
Like a compass, a cracked cowbell sat
On the dashboard, its black mouth a contradiction,
One lip curled North, the other South
Like a griot's or seashell's. Young Boy
Doubled as driver & navigator—
A dirty windshield like a veil,
The only thing between him & myth.

2

Suburbia was mysterious,
Calmer, less poetic. The homes were armless,
Flat & wide, unable to reach up
Or out like most prose. Stars hid
Like schools of truant fish,
The headlights in their moist skulls
Blinking off & on, distress signals,
Gossip from God. A cop's flashlight
Stood in for the moon,
A navel holding together heaven.

3

After we cranked,
They grooved and the ladies
We thought had come to see us
Drifted beyond our reach. That night,
Names & numbers were exchanged,
Directions drawn on the blank maps
Of palms. Also, something as out
Of reach as dawn broke in us
And our shadows tried to climb sky
The wrong way down.

Tambourine Tommy

More man
Than myth, more myth
Than freak, he would come out,
Between bands,

In a harness of bells
And high waters,
Held together and up
By a belt of rope.

His skin was thick
As friendship, his spotlit scalp
Clean as the repaired dome
Of the U.S. Capitol.

Rickety raw
And rickety strong,
He'd run from Barry Farms
To Mount Vernon

With bricks
Borrowed from the wall
Around St. Elizabeths Hospital
In each hand.

There was struggle
In his dance,
Like first-of-the-month
Or Election Day downtown.

His arms tried to
Free Terrance Johnson,
His trickster legs
Rayful Edmond.

But such drama
Never made him more
Than spectacle or more
Than beast.

No one thought
Of him as artist,
No one thought
Of him as activist.

His craft, the way
He beat himself
(head, shoulders, knees
And toes), proved he

Was one of us,
A soul searcher
Born and raised
In the District,

Proved he
Could reach in,
Blend, ease before entering,
Proved he

Was our phoenix,
Nobody's Stonestreet,
Part hustler, part athlete,
Tougher than all of Southeast.

Fatal April

Thomas Leon Ellis, Sr. (1945–1991)

The phone rang. It was Doris,
Your sister, calling to say
April had taken you, where,
In your bedroom, when, days ago,
How, murder, no, a stroke.

You left a car (but I
Don't drive) and enough cash
In your pockets to buy
A one-way train ticket
From Boston to Washington.

Let's get one thing straight.
I didn't take the money, but
I did take your driver's license
And the Chuck Brown album,
Needle to groove,

Round and round,
Where they found you.
Both were metaphors.
The license I promised, but knew
I'd never get—now I have yours

And the album because
Of what you may have been
Trying to say about writing,
About home. James keeps
Asking me to visit your grave,

When will I learn to drive
And why I changed my name.
He's your son, stubborn with
An inherited temper. I keep telling him
No, never, there's more than

One way to bury a man.

THOMAS SAYERS ELLIS

View of the Library of Congress
from Paul Laurence Dunbar High School

For Doris Craig and Michael Olshausen

A white substitute teacher
At an all-Black public high school,
He sought me out saying my poems
Showed promise, range, a gift,
And had I ever heard of T.S. Eliot?
No. Then Robert Hayden perhaps?

Hayden, a former colleague,
Had recently died, and the obituary
He handed me had already begun
Its journey home—from the printed page
Back to tree, gray becoming
Yellow, flower, dirt.

No river, we skipped rocks
On the horizon, above Ground Zero,
From the roof of the Gibson Plaza Apartments.
We'd aim, then shout the names
Of the museums, famous monuments,
And government buildings

Where our grandparents, parents,
Aunts, and uncles worked. Dangerous duds.
The bombs we dropped always fell short,
Missing their mark. No one, not even
Carlton Green who had lived in
As many neighborhoods as me,

Knew in which direction
To launch when I lifted Hayden's
Place of employment—

The Library of Congress—
From the obituary, now folded
In my back pocket, a creased map.

We went home, asked our mothers
But they didn't know. Richard's came
Close: Somewhere near Congress,
On Capitol Hill, take the 30 bus,
Get off before it reaches Anacostia,
Don't cross the bridge into Southeast.

The next day in school
I looked it up—the National Library
Of the United States in Washington, D.C.
Founded in 1800, open to all taxpayers
And citizens. *Snap!* My Aunt Doris
Works there, has for years.

Once, on her day off, she
Took me shopping and bought
The dress shoes of my choice.
Loafers. They were dark red,
Almost purple, bruised—the color
Of blood before oxygen reaches it.

I was beginning to think
Like a poet, so in my mind
Hayden's dying and my loafers
Were connected, but years apart,
As was Dunbar to other institutions—
Ones I could see, ones I could not.

Larissa Szporluk

Prowler's Universe

LARISSA SZPORLUK was born in 1967 in Ann Arbor, Michigan. She studied at the Iowa Writers' Workshop and holds degrees from the University of Michigan, the University of California at Berkeley, and the University of Virginia (where she was a Henry Hoyns fellow). She teaches at Bowling Green State University and is completing her second collection of poems, *Dark Sky Question*.

For my parents

Koan

You cross a broken field.
Mirror, mirror.
There's a scarecrow in a dress.

Sometimes I know
I won't see you again.
It's a bad place

to get emotional, alone
in the car, haze pouring
through the valley.

But I see you on your knees,
I see everything,
her stick arms pull you

to her skirt, hens
seeking shelter, I hear
crying. I hear crying

as the only true noise,
a chorus of tearing ice,
the dead straw

she is made of
crying, crows caught
in the sky, a duct

of her odd world;
in your rush to get in,
you bruise the shape

of your being.
This window I look out of
traps my breath

until nothing I pound
isn't part mine,
and black-and-blue inside.

Allegro of the Earth

It takes many doves to make a woman.
I've been chasing them forever
as they drift through summer unexplained.
Like the need in certain sounds
to be fulfilling, they repeat each year
blue fields, blue frost, far north,
ferried across gulfs,
in search of the torturer's house;
miles away, he unlocks his clear interior door.
I lose them to him every time.
Don't cry. Be warm. Watch how.
And as he changes them completely,
peeling them down
to the hollow that resides at the center
of all of them, a piccolo hole,
the sole shape of his desire,
a hollow that listens,
shivers, ringing the dim light,
arrested by their separated feathers,
I'm aware of one thing.

Prowler's Universe

i

Everything is mine for a while.
Her chest gives pause to what her life is.
I could use a stick to make it louder.

I could be her family, lift her by the hips
from this roof and watch her fly,
borne by the lie of trust

between us—there is no pond,
no wreck, no bottom . . .
The smear that is her cheek,

sidelong, sedate,
rides the surface near the shore now.
I feel her with my knees:

She grows big like glass and I
am Spring and the mind
is just the woman we're all after.

ii

In the beginning, she is afraid
of the cattle.
They are not from the heart.
They shake a little rain or something on her face.

She twitches from sounds that pass
through her blood
of a faraway, then close, then far, entourage.
Not a colorful xylophone sound

but hard, like a game
under stadium lights. When the land jerks,
she jerks, moist and reddish,
with the land . . .

gets used to the licking,
throws her pants up like a kite—
her smile survives.
No era is spared the site of her lips

as she gives, smiling,
her body's tiny organisms
to occidental winds
to be ruptured. *Do good. Serve. Give.*

iii

For five minutes,
there was dust—of voices,
structures within structures,
cosmos, whatever it was,
the face it cost.

When will I give up
my love of pain?
When I am equal to the whole world.
When I roll over,
and the empty sky is perfect.

Under the Bridge

You never know when somebody will
stick a little knife
in your heart and walk away —

and the handle that smells of his hand
vibrates by your breast
as he ducks through the trees

and minutes later blows like a shirt pin
across the frozen lake.
And you're all wet, and he's in love

with what he's done.
And because of the cut,
the distance of your life pours out,

and because of the clouds
like fat that surround you,
you don't hear

for a long time
the tom-tom beating
in the sky, letting shadows

too heavy to be birds,
and yelling with a message
to forgive him

like the others did their father
under that bridge there
where ropes still linger

in remembrance of their necks,
where a flute in its case lies cold—
forgive him. Say

his name. It was only
power that he had to have,
and look what the one thrust gave him.

Avalanche

Look toward the snow,
its hurry to disappear,
to treat the Earth lightly,

then toward your daughter
to see if she's the stranger
race of air. She either

hates the mountain weather,
or likes it too much,
that it has to be paid for

with her life, so you can watch
God whip night around,
lose sight of her coat,

call her name into the space
that hasn't seen her, or anyone,
and isn't lonely.

You won't want to find her
until it's just too late,
the omniscience on her face

an afterglow below the rubble
you'll imagine through
to feel what barely lived,

a chronology already swallowed;
she was your satellite
and had to be spun away,

far from where the truth lies
that you kept quiet
as everything slid and slid.

Radiolaria

Maybe the earth where her house is
is dangerous,
the foundation easing away.

She's out of the man.
Bereavement means travel, nearly,
a plane with no wings,

her face on the rug,
moment of confusion:
But I asked him to leave,

he was stretching . . .
Slush in the lowlands.
It must have been an old

attachment. Something
outside of her is thinking,
I didn't even feel him;

she was drawn down.
Her vowels went dark.
Her body rowed back

to a time when loss
was not yet architecture,
but still on the eyes

as the weight that would make
her want to build,
when rocks opened up,

and small lives within,
and within, opened up,
until their skins filled the water,

and rose to the sun realm.
Maybe she rose with them,
and landed here, as they flew on,

and like their broken skeletons,
she's staying flat
to grow elaborate again.

Round Face in a Little Town

Holy one. What does the vine
teach the tree
about adornment,

about slow choking
in the forest, the forced
together-bend,

or the willing to
because the sun feels weirdly
daring as it ends?

Because the swan boats
have rusted, at last they can cry
their boredom. He pushes

you forward, your clothes
blowing north, hair
pulled, roots

in your sex, the scoop
of your back made deeper
like a melon—

I ask because you know.
Your arms might resist,
but loosely,

like a newborn's
twisting on a bed,
and he smiles then

because life has to climb
if nothing else,
and there's nothing else

around to climb. You will be
remembered by that pond,
what your body was

doing to amuse him,
for how quickly
you could adjust,

as if to a sudden twin,
loving the room it occupies,
the winding up

to be pedalled again,
too young to be degraded
and stay put.

Bluebells

Bared too, I take a risk
in coming out here.
This is the war summer.

Clowns really shake
in the stutter
of low-flying airplanes.

Above, my light jacket
hangs from the tree
like Vivienne's

decision (while her father
cracked nuts—
Come home soon!).

At midnight I'll leave
with earth on my face,
but for now I am down

for the strange
digging that men do,
for the quick trust

I feel in the sky,
like a guest book
signed by a loner,

and the wild interplay
below of a missing
girl's soul moving

unseen past roots
and time. I think of
the clothes. Of the giant

dislike that smells
the new blood inside me,
of a child at recess,

bent from making
love, who finds
what the rain worms acquire.

Solar Wind

I don't pray.
I just walk out there
where it's thin
with my bow and aim.

But I should have yelled.
I should have changed the world.

A person can die of balance,
just gleam like squid
and disappear.

The fence around our house
is soft with rain.
It can't stop my arrows.
It can't stop

what wants to happen,
the meteors I hear, power lines
blowing from the mountain,

or the girl somewhere
who reads you,
whose skin has memorized your life.
Nothing stops her fingers;
they swim with you at night.

Leave if you're leaving.
Leave plain mud.

I don't know what else
is on your beard.
It would be mercy, God.

I grow weird in the field.

The Bystander's Power

The man won't need to rise
from his hammock to know
the size of the body riding the roan.

He'll just rub his eyes
behind the black patches,
and through the pin drizzle

hear thighs
sliding on the animal. His mind,
like spore along the trail,

loses not one sound,
not of the toad sapped
underhoof, not of the girl's

seventh hiccup.
Aroused on his rope bed,
the man can prod them on

toward a crack-claimed
tunnel no longer frequented
by trains and feel,

therein, the tail slap
off rain, and cheer
the consummation of their yell

as they cease to see the light
of the violet-strewn meadow
that by logic had to follow,

and cheer their echo
as they cease to reappear.
And when his own heart has properly

cooled, he will peel away
the patches, glad
that her soul after all

was such a small
thing, a paper boat
degrading into pulp, a mild

irritant at sea.
And he is glad of the truth
of conception—that two kinds

of babies always grow.
So he smiles in the least
fantastic way now, a measured

lack of hurry, as it is
with men who lurk at stables,
the whiskey in their eyes

guessing how far they might go
in their boots across the dust
to meet their ugliest selves.

Envoy of the Boat

He loves what he cannot love,
lapping toward it, with the love
that exists between lakes, wanting each other
so much, wanting just to meet
inside themselves, taste the fish,
how deep is your gulch,
how vocal the fowl that visit you?
With unexpected tenderness,
that's how he lives, watching,
dreaming at night they grow close,
the forlorn part of their bodies
upswelling with swell, each pore frothed too,
morning forgotten, the message, war,
more sky in his mouth than water.

Benefits of Drowning

The light has been so awful.
Not whipped as a child,
I'm scared of human power.
They say there is an end
but I go round and round
with unscrupulous desires
in regions of my throat.
Nests smell from neglect.
Autumn will smell too
if the summer wasn't good.
Hard rain brings exaltation.
All the little mouths come out,
blowing rings of brightness.
I can enter them, not stagger,
not a skeleton, not plagued,
not by ghosts.

Ideogram

The worm will turn
toward the beech trees.
The girl will turn toward the body
she first knew. A stranger's.
Father's. A brother's friend's.
To face the thing itself.
The beech trees stand in the light
diseased. The hermaphrodite
crawls. She makes peace
with him who wants her.

The wonderful power of the mind
to build a maze for little
individuals. Look at the figure
with scratched knees picking
berries from the hedgerow,
poisonous and sweet: Run,
Petria Amos! a higher voice yells,
Run for your life! But she can't see;
the corners keep cutting into more—
Remember what your mother said!

About twilight. Not to believe
the absolute loneliness of the driver
of the blue car. Not to believe
that his door might not open.
That the lamb in his yard
is real—you will never feel
its living tongue. But there is
sleep, says the voice, if you swallow
the pictures as they come;
the awful ones last the least long.

Devolution

She raises her arm and spills sand
and looks back at you
and you're looking too. Dalmatians
flash by like spliced
time and you feel dizzy.

Her father crowds the towel.
His brow shines. His trunks unwrinkle
where his groin works with a dream—
people disappoint you from inside:
Spiderwebs thrive

in space they can't fill, whose oscillations
feel like whipping sounds, like horses
being punished far away, or tires
on new tar. She may look beautiful
in long green hiking shorts

and climb as high as a man,
but as soon as you accost her,
which you will, the silk
will drop through the dark as you had feared,
and though she has consented,

web is all you feel:
You might smell her forever, the ginger ale
she is drinking, bad sea
in her hair, but it's stretching, the wind gap—
where her breasts were is desert.

Libido

A hand has her hair.
Don't move, don't cry out—
The odd foliage is shining in the light.

With the stealth of a wheel,
he rams against her knees
from behind. She falls

back into his purpose,
which is hers: to be provided for,
to find her insides altered

and grow huge.
But he runs off, done with her mouth,
leaving her dazed by the waste

of that kind of love.
She asks around, asks how,
where do we feel to find who we are,

watches some poppies freeze
in an orgy of plants,
their cold red gaze grown sideways.

She listens to parrots,
true inner birds, never at rest,
into whose breasts the world

blows pleasure,
shaking like nests full of Indian bees—
To scream is to sing.

A Cappella

They were lying in the shoreline
foam, navels
trapping sand, eyes open
on the pebbles and the tiny spiral
shells, and he turned to him and said,
Did you love much?

He squeezed a slippy sea grub.
Not much.

And it was quiet. Undivided
quiet. Even the great
claws of tide
tore into them in silence.

This is how it is, they guessed,
to run out of fresh
ideas . . .

Heed the jellyfish, the first man mouthed,
Float more still-ly.
But his words weren't loud,

and the other man grabbed it,
a fat one, lilac,
and everything formerly dumb
broke — like divas
into octaves as he underwent alone.

LARISSA SZPORLUK

Price of Ruin

A rib cage lies
in the snow, almost
immaculate.

You crouch
to listen to the wind
scan each bone

with the know-how
of a falcon.
For thirteen hours,

we've said nothing.
Ice builds
around our eyes.

I've been thinking
how huge
exists in miniature,

my recurring
nightmare of a wolf
inside a shell,

unable to kill moose
but planning in its tight
spiral prison

something crueller,
from which they'll crave
their own removal.

Anhedonia

Deciduous trees sleep well in winter.
There are fewer hives,
decreasing rivalries and flutter.
Those who die, die from work,
holding something snowy up,
a formula, a gin, a comb.
Between pain and recovery
is an insane soft light, a fur
that ceases to protect;
fated to the eyes of people,
it twists to get away from them,
loved by them, lost in them.
Incest keeps the world going
until it's time, once again, to freeze,
during which all peace is bred,
in retrospect, things he said:
Your breasts are full of heron feathers,
hoard of my wild life.

Quiet Emergency

Sun, come a little closer.
They need you.
Their tights are loose and muddied.

Sun, come and be good-looking,
like the angel Michael.
Promise them

snacks. What they've been through
they've grown cold in
self-defense of.

Lying so wonderfully gentle,
borne by the grass,
their arms appear yearning

now to fly — really fast
they'd go in order
to forget the negligent

mother Earth.
In the air there's a different
dynamic. It's

broader. The impulse
to harm, if it ever was, is
less

construed. All that's being
said here, on this
page

is that they're damp.
Like fresh, cut
herbs. And it's not a helicopter

they require, but a yellow,
somewhat medical
zeal.

Age of Piracy

They reach through her brow
to tear out the trees
they think she dreams about,
the balanced land she left behind,
and throw her boat back,
empty, to him she left behind,
and laugh at her mistake,
that she could fly on and on,
out of their sight and knowledge.
And they laugh into life
beyond themselves, as she, obsessed,
stares up at the dipping sky,
past the spreading pitch, telling herself,
I am that high, and they laugh
as they open what they stole,
seeing nothing was in her but sea
and the long tedium of falling,
lost in her green and winding galleries,
tucks and turns, and they laugh,
wings in their teeth beating backwards.

Agnosia

A far star is making leaves.
Someday they might brush this place,
their ordinary fire

tittering around us.
The porches are locked at dusk.
A piece could be out there.

But you should think less,
how you threw yourself on her back,
and the voice of the wharf's

weak-looking birds cried
more than it had to, the dark red dress
falling ill. And you blew

all the animals away,
and never stopped feeling their dirt.
You ran after her too,

for a year, on your skeleton foot
over the hollow ice,
to prove to yourself

what was left
the cannibal wind would be finishing
up, the tail end

of her solved in the sky,
how an enemy bends,
a girl, water jug, edges adjusting in time.

Swordfish Season

Summer suffers most without a daughter.
There are seven octaves to obey,
do, re, mi. Without her, there's no order;
water freezes, *sol, la, fa,*
in mid-massage, walls of Jericho crumble,
seven stories, seven shocks.
The men who used to come here,
drawn to her narrow spot, aimed at getting through,
until the deep sea found a way,
shadows cutting murk—the sword
entered gradually, widening the halo
in her eye, and halted, an inch inside her body,
si, inaudible to ears, taking control,
great control, *do,* killing instantly.

Krell

He arrives and looks around,
and doesn't know the word for wind,
and wind is the subject.

He finds a girl on a fence
hurting herself with a nail.
He pulls her away without speaking,

to her surprise, and wipes
the stuff from her hair that smells
like burning-out lights,

and suddenly it's not a burden
to be walking with her
in enemy land. When she tells him

"the best thing here is the moon,"
he feels happier than if he'd seen it
and remembers a parable

about a string that never meets
its ends, and she tells him then
about a warm place at the end

of a grove of horned trees.
If the night steadies, if it controls
their speed, they'll reach it

together, fusing in the meantime,
discarding all the nuance
that betrays them with disease.

Gemini

In the world of our room,
there is one light.
We sit under it.

I'm reading about tumors;
you, about Rome, in German.
I see my hairs on the rug

like old territorial secrets,
a web in regress,
multiple lostness.

The Case of the Terrible
Tumor: The victim rode his bike
as fast as he could

into the wall of his school!
Children gathered
at the wreck of him.

Pedals spinning, broken
head! Blood brings
pleasure to everything,

as flowers do,
blooming out of season.
They watched it spread,

pulsing, on the grass.
Somebody lifted the frame,
found a hand, and held it,

as if to hold every opposite,
every spirit, body, end
and beginning, intact.

Mauvaises Terres

The world could only be a ship,
a hunted thing to the pale light,
a swerving single body,
broken in the act and in the echo
of suggestion. With her strange fidelity
to dead and lonely sunsets, she heads
for what the dreamer in the dark
had first intended, airless chasms,
smiling depressions. If there had been
a chance, an intelligence, floating
in the wake, if only it had whispered
with the integer of a voice,
or finger, *Don't let me down,*
Earth would have heard the sound
unfinished mother, and reared her prow
in wonder that this was her son, *wait,*
that his life would urge legends,
it's my turn, of the love she had made.

Ignis Fatuus

I can't cope in the bog light.
I was made big and not great.

Moths swarmed in from the plains,
wings of all sizes.

And to think that I did the same,
half-cry of a star

whose boundaries were torn,
then your special way of walking

on the peels. Beautiful voiceless things
were boiled alive.

For three thousand days, I asked you
to stop it.

Little girls are scarcer now.
There won't be a second bride.

Who could go on trying?
Victims form a line even God doesn't know,

their desire for home
snuffed out like a phantom.

I'll catch silk in the night wind instead,
narrations of our baby.

Part of the sky is all of the sky.
The rest is wasted.

Meat, Jealousy, and the Sun

I know the look of need in a field,
having been filled once.
It is not right.

Every night the bats turn ageless,
chase each other,
panting in the shingles.

Another globe leaves your body.
It's slow, rubbing the window
with red light.

Where were they during your life?
We made love the last time
in a voice not quite ours,

the globe soaring out
the next dawn too strong
for any human to have hosted.

* * *

I wasn't sure about the ending.
There are mornings like that.
The sky can't get out
of what happened at night.
The adjustment is too large.

There was a flush,
and a group cry.
Then your plane flew away,
and there was no hesitation
on your part—

but we only just met,
so it must have been the ad
for the open-air museum that sparked it.
Besides, most people aren't in love;
their eyes are just full.

But I felt in my back
that you lived,
you really lived,
and down the power of dream
will retravel me.

Ghost Continent

It's a lot like emptiness, the season
of dying fish, black drink,
the person you loved best, and left,
giving off light in the recession.
It would have startled the fire user,
who towered over nature,
this material you're passing through
to save a little of, like a radio.
Paddle faster. Skim across the giant
things in hiding, blow on the sick.
The deep returns a makeshift
surface, wake, blue-tarred road.
Miles from here (but you're gone)
the wrong land will be discovered.

Joe Osterhaus

The Domed Road

JOE OSTERHAUS was born in Cleveland, Ohio. He grew up in the Midwest and California and received a B.A. from Pomona College and an M.A. from the University of Chicago. His essays and poems have appeared in *AGNI*, the *Antioch Review*, *Bostonia*, the *Boston Review*, the *Formalist*, the *Journal*, and the *Nebraska Review*. He has worked for several scholarly publishers and taught at Boston University. He currently serves as the poetry review editor for *AGNI*, and works in the Boston area as a technical writer.

These poems are dedicated to my teachers,
Bob Jarnigan, Bob Mezey, Robert Pinsky, and Derek Walcott,
whose inspiration made them possible;
and to Erin,
who is the syllable that rhymes with life.

Where have I been this while exiled from thee?
BEN JONSON

JOE OSTERHAUS

The Owl

So Hegel's Owl of Minerva spreads
its wings at sundown, beginning its long flight
when depth and outline are the most obscure —
how true the image is, yet how unclear,
as if the thinker wanted both the night
and the raptor's shadow gliding over the dry beds.

Pepper

I can't remember why I stepped outside,
but on the walk I took the camera
and, in the bluing air, with a backward stride,
aligned the moment in the aperture.

Now as I hold the picture, I recall
the heat of the evening; my flushed skin;
how, after stepping from the unlit hall,
I turned back to the voices talking within.

Beneath the sprawling arbor of the porch
my parents and the neighbors end the day
as the blue smoke from a mosquito torch
pours from its orange canister, and thins away.

They're seated at a rickety deal table
from which a late-night meal has just been cleared,
my father, leaning forward on an elbow,
arguing some point in a day-old beard.

Not to be outdone, our neighbor eyes
his swelling bloodlines as my father speaks,
and, as he finishes, laughs, and replies
that Nixon will survive the *Post*'s critiques.

My mother and her best friend listen, flushed
with the white wine, whose level, taut and clear,
rides the bottle's waist. Within a year,
her tumor having burst, her family hushed,

the friend will lie in a coma in the hospital.
Her manner in the photo thus takes on
the preordaining nature of a spell,
her gesture, grimace, thought both limned and drawn.

My parents, too, already sit apart,
gesticulating as they have for days,
while, at their feet, a child with a toy cart
toils through the steeps as they avoid my gaze.

Along with anger, a lesson passes on,
as, spying from a cloud of netted flowers,
the children hide, eyes clear with exhaustion,
and taste the sexual liquor of the hour.

And I can't doubt their laughter, or the ease
with which the families lounge after their meal;
the pool, reflected, chafed by a light breeze;
the dachshunds begging at my father's heel.

See how the cellar at the table's edge,
inconsequential then, lets go a drift
of black grains that swarm over the image,
with love and incoherence in the rift.

The Ironists

But something, too, is lost: the small boy with hair
the color of sand, who, eating an apple in the doorway
of an old house, hears the split oak creak in the wind,
a door closing in the pantry, and finally the chime

his mother's laughter makes, as she takes her place
across the table from a bearded man, who asks
if the boy usually ignores the bell, then lights
the long, wind-guttered taper, hand dipped briefly in the flame.

Quiver

In the green room, our teacher filled the board
with a vocabulary taken from
the water-colored myths we'd soon begin:
quiver, oxen, loam, and *sounding board;*
aurora, dawn, Olympus, sweet reward.
Shifting in our chairs at each new word,
we listened as she spoke above the sounds
of a classmate beating the erasers clean
on the brick wall next to the playground stair
and a latecomer, running over the grounds,
who spun the rusted carousel as he flew past.

One word catches in my mind: *quiver,*
and I think of an angel with its bow,
the black quills bristling like nerves when plucked
out of the taut, sky blue interior—
and in this light his targets show the mark
of a concentration foreign to the class;
the held-breath concentration of an addict
holding a match beneath a blackening spoon:
Matt, with a black eye caught from a swing;
Tony, brooding in an endless, inner way
about his half sister's leukemia;
Jeff, grinning as he swings the misshapen hand
for which he is admired, feared, and mocked.

Before we ever thought we might discuss
the losses in the stories as events
we could relate to what would change in us,
Mrs. Derringer set down her book
and said she'd soon wipe the chalkboard clean
as, too young to have imagined our own deaths,
we gazed back like the scholars in the grove.

The Domed Road

At night, as I turn through the empty rooms
and straighten up cups and shoes and chairs,
I always finish, as my mother did,
by standing briefly in the kitchen door
where, as the tap gleams with the street's one light
and the refrigerator pops and whines,
I place my glasses on the countertop
and turn back through the open door to bed.
Sometimes, in the split, ramshackle haze
of my myopia, in which the walls
seem almost to thrill with an animal life,

a doubt begins as I stare through the dark:
in the winged shadow of a Morris chair
or the banked cyclone of an Oriental rug
I gain a vantage point
from which my waking life seems harsh and small,
as if, in looking forward to my dreams,
I suddenly looked back through eye and mind
to find my life was wrong,
then found the traces of a larger, subtler life
like the sharp taste of ether in the mouth.
Even in the day that life will seek

the crazed, erratic jots of nothingness
that unfold like a coal mine in the air —
the coral fissures in the walk; the moss
rising like a cloud on a split fence —
and trace in them the pressure of that night
where we were spun from calcium and dread.
But who would stop the workings of that mind
when it can also trace a memory

to its progenitor in an old house,
the latter shaken by the passing cars
and the odd peal of thunder through the rain.

Often, when a boy, I wondered why
she left her glasses several rooms away;
why, on turning in, she didn't think
to set them on the nightstand near her bed,
for reading or just staring through the dark.
It seems now she left them there in faith,
to show she'd so surrendered to her house
that, late at night, should she be called awake,
she needn't bother to distinguish things
from the soiled shadows that they cast,
or catch the moonglint on the patio

whitening the gloss of our lost selves.
Something willful, too, in that thickening
of the already close-knit atmosphere
first taught me as I came back home at night
from heated bouts of flashlight tag, or, later,
from the domed roads of cannabis and sex
of how we manage to accept our lives —
to leave one's glasses on the countertop
so far from where one slept, turned out to be
a promise that the day would come
when all the rooms would wear the same starched black.

The Invisible Man

In the grainy, late-night science fiction film
the scientist discovers how to bend the laws
of light, until, one night, he strips away the gauze
to find himself the master of a nonce realm.
Yet he remains intent upon his recent life
and haunts the walkways of the planetarium
where soldiers pick him out with searchlights on the dome
as a querulous shadow folded in upon itself.
Crazed when he discovers flesh is memory
in the final moments he swings upon a stair
while, awaiting his faint image in the glare,
the soldiers aim the cannon and small weaponry
at nothing, and fire when a breeze gives him away—
struck, he waxes back, and stares through lowered eyes
at the faint tinge of blood welling like cowardice
from a thin crook of wind, as if at last to say
invisibility gave even love its place.
And so, the soldiers stepping forward in a ring,
the human trace grown stronger with his vanishing
led a junior officer to veil that face.

After Borges

for Robert Mezey

No matter how well read the students are,
they'll never read the periodicals
that lined the shelves some twenty years before
and had a shorter half-life in the stalls —

pulp flowers from midwestern college towns
with faded blue insignia, and type
that wanders where the paper cracks and browns
and in the margins takes a challenge up.

Experience itself diminishes,
the authors' very earnestness the cause,
and as the barnyard swallows loop and chase
blueflies and midges at the evening's close,

we hear Theocritus's nightingale
like water through the dense air of a well.

Tomis

Ovid, exiled, wrote his *Tristia*
to plead with Caesar in the capital;
though he'd once written some erotica
his conduct since had been impeccable,
save one transgression he can't bring himself to name,
more out of seeming reticence than shame.

And, as he makes his case, one notices
how clear the task was in his mind: to prove
to Augustus, and then Tiberius,
that he deserved their pardon, if not love,
and, reinstated, would help advance
those subtle arts most often left to chance.

In this, his case was different from ours,
who face, instead of kings, indifference;
that has as many faces as the slow hours
and braids its criticism without sense,
yet still consigns the writer to a spring
of thick ice, brown water, and slow blossoming.

And if we wonder what he did, what act
turned king and court against him in the end,
the scholars, with their customary tact,
cite several possibilities, that blend
slender intrigues of moonlight and complaint—
we do know, when accused, he showed restraint.

Exiled, Ovid sealed his world in wax:
flowers sprouting unevenly from frost and mold;
the harbor sliding under a mist that stacks
the slate gray vistas into hill and fold;
the packed earth of the village; the boarskin drum;
the hails of poisoned arrows and tedium.

And in his Rome, the insolent white light
still floods the courtyards in the afternoon,
where courtiers mock a youthful anchorite
and fix their boredom on the waning moon;
their studied conversation and bald lies
made timeless by the plain white balconies.

Piecework

for Erin

My lover works at a computer screen,
the letters and the green fields they compose
varying their strata until they glean
associations from the shining rows.

And as she works, how intimate becomes
the space between the rippling monitor
and her bent head—as the small fan hums,
she bends forward, lost to its spark and whir.

The space we both require to compose
is different for each: I need low light,
coffee, the cut-off grain of wood or rows
of books, while you need just a space so bright

it naturally inclines you toward the screen
and all the variations hid between.

The Coast Road

Perspective, when it's noticed, bears the weight
of everything that's brought you to that point;
so, on the coast road, where the green cliffs mount
the channel from a rumpled length of slate,
you waste the moment feeling fortunate.

The ocean, toiling like an image through cracked paint,
tears on the rocks, then closes where a cormorant
fits the contours of the mountains to the wind
by leveling the whitecaps in the mind.
The moon, thinned to near transparence by the mist,

churns on the ocean at a deeper level
and, pivoting on nothing, lets nothing waste —
the same moon that on other nights witnessed
the tangling of our limbs and the swaying post,
a white smudge the waves thin and unravel —

typically, we didn't meet till ten,
and, exhausted, talked very little —
taking the blankets from the old oak settle,
we'd find such solace as was promised then,
and stop only if the doorknob rattled.

The last time I was there, I didn't know
I'd never visit in that way again,
complaining of my work, the streets, the rain;
and, looking back, I still don't know
what I was thinking of; how I could have been so vain.

To an Aborted Child

Once, when your father was vacationing
in London, he stopped for dinner in a restaurant
on a side street in Piccadilly,
an empty place with closed-off banquet rooms
and waiters with a grim, resilient tact.
The decor was Scottish, the food Indian,
and, nearly penniless, your father took
his own sweet time in ordering, then chose
the cheapest dinner item he could pick
off the soiled menu. From where he sat he heard
the door to the men's room banging shut; the shriek
of rusted pulleys as the kitchen help
threw pans back on the shelves; and the murmuring
of the waiters behind a thin partition.
The meal itself was unexceptional,
nourishing yet bland, and the dark ale
was still on his breath in Garrick's Theatre
where he sat level with the chandelier,
the clicking of its dust-covered facets
as dry and distant as the waiter's voice.

Please know your father loved you and didn't want
to bring you half-prepared into the world;
that he thought of you incessantly, if you count
his worrying about his time and place,
which I do; that he wanted you to know
each corner of the city that baffled him
and taste the victories that he enjoyed,
even the small: the bad meals in cheap diners;
the inexpensive entertainments bought
on credit, without thought, and soon forgot
till the creditors came banging at the door.
Please know that when like yours his time came due
your father wasn't bitter; that he was at last

grateful for each chance to see the day
end in a tumult of cloud-light over the roads;
and that, of all the alternating lives
he tried on and threw off; of all the days
he lived well and then forgot at night,
the days when he decided your sweet fate
came back to him too charged, too sweet, too full.

Sweet Decision

Out walking one night, I overheard
a man saying to a woman that
he hadn't made his mind up when she called

but now was almost ready to decide.
And I was skeptical: so often when
we're ready to decide, we just fall back,

till predilection, masked as choice, decides —
a true decision is as rare as love.
Still, the dialogue persists, the slow

admission and rethinking of the thick
white horns of the sea beast in the dream; the rare
trapped bird with blood and gene-flecks in its eyes;

and if these creatures grow too mythical
with their faint chirrs and swarming in the tomb
the endlessness of the dialogue remains,

its pattern like the repetition of
the man speaking to the woman in the doorway,
his foot on the step as he looks up at her,

and the sea behind them rising at the docks,
as if to claim once and for all the rust
and silver moonglint on the ships and rails.

The Long Afternoon

for Sally Brickell and Jeff Kaplan

Here the friendship lies in everything not said—
living alone, one learns to hide remorse
by bartering one's silence on that head
for something deftly original, or worse.

And there are certain stories I won't tell,
such as combing the tangles from her hair
while she dug in a basket for a gel,
and then that heavy scent beading the air,

or, on a long afternoon we spent in bed,
the sweetness as I refused my otherness
and love evaporated to a giddy dread
as the rain fell from a sky green as glass.

But friends can only follow one so far—
closing the door behind you in the hall
they leave you, as they should, to find your car
amid the darkened arches of the mall.

Pact

The fringed noise of the shot: he slumps, struck in the brow.
His eyes grow vacant and a sash of blood
refuses to be tied across his forehead—
willing herself to follow, she says *now*

and turns the black revolver on herself—
but, somehow, the wind in a broken tree
and all the branches tossing in the gulf
shatter the space of their complicity,

and in that space she hears another wind
raking pebbles and weeds in the steep arroyo.
Knowing she's betrayed him in her mind,
she opens the car door, swings her feet to the rough gravel,

and looks down on the hemisphere of light.
When her time comes, she goes alone, in spite.

The Return

If I go bankrupt as the cratered moon,
buoyed by debts whose burnt foils brimmed with light,
and leave my creditors with just the tune
of indignation swinging through the night,

I promise to return to them and you
the gist of what I borrowed: sun on wood,
green leaf, white stone, the scent of coffee, dew,
the sheen of ardor, and the smell of cooking food;

the broad red cellar door; the beat of wind
on a green outcrop above a bearing gulf;
the conversation with a stranger in a bar
who clearly didn't want to know herself;

the songs and books; the clock tower whose bell
spilled bright, clipped tones; the goat farm and shy kids
the day the farmhands herded them uphill
to that ruddy house with tendons on the skids;

the engine running smoothly, and then rough;
the slow train, cut-out landscapes, and deep yards;
the cheap seats in the theater, and the bluff
I never could bring off with the wrong cards;

the beach fire and pillowed sand; the stars
blotted first by smoke and then by sleep;
the beaded ligatures and feathered scars
whose edges shone like flaked salt in the deep;

the evenings spent alone; the mornings wrung
from aimlessness over a half-read book;
the perfumes and colognes so harsh they stung;
the part-time jobs from editor to cook;

the leather wingtips, silver cuff links, silk
and cotton shirts; the patterns on the ties
changing like leaves along the downtown walk,
each season bearing its identities;

I give them back to you, the interest
I took in them now withered at the root,
and whatever creditor picks through the rest
will know of me just rumor and black soot—

if disapproval, flourished like a brush,
paints my failures a proliferating red,
say that I sought a carelessness as harsh
as a new moon lodged in an abandoned shed.

The Habit of Money

That spring, the weather and the new-leaved trees
were of the same consistency: thin, bright,
with surfaces so sharp they cracked the glaze
flaked from our sleep's annealing trance at night.

Things slowed, as people saw in one another
the same beleaguered wonder at the day—
a grace it had, devouring all others,
like the white sparks in an arc welder's bouquet.

I traded nothing to break free that spring
and watched the weather change through the dark glass
of cars and offices, till, lengthening,
the days were wrapped in summer's heat and dross.

And, in the sea green hour before the rain,
the trees paid out that flimsy silver coin.

Husk

Chambered house; deep hedge; riverglint through trees;
the open book of day, so closely read
that in the livid characters one sees
the undertow unmaking every bed;

this summer, I had promised to forget
those contrapuntal phantoms, age and wealth;
but not the aurora and its cold jet
or the blaze and chevrons on the whales, whose stealth

when tracing a song's weight
we witnessed as a thrashing in the troughs —
and from this prospect, it's not too late;
we'll sit at the long table, chafing the husks

till the shot silk lies scattered on the floor,
and the moon lights the blisters on the door.

The Hook

Considering the thirties, one should note
how well the propagandists did their work —
so well, that we can only now remark
those hidden excesses that won the vote;

they were that closely tied. And now, possessed
by everyone who's felt the glamour of
those backlit scenes where Garbo swore off love,
those years sport our affection like a crest.

When will the dangers of that time, its rank
political hysterias, refute
our fierce nostalgia for its airbrushed look —

perhaps the crimson banners and bright tanks,
the newsreel footage of the young recruit
with such untroubled eyes, must bait the hook.

JOE OSTERHAUS

Shall We Dance

In *Shall We Dance*, the thirties musical
in which Astaire and Rogers play
a pair of lovestruck impresarios
who can't, it seems for the entire film,
admit they care for one another, time
itself is present in the scenes, shifting
the burden of their style to what they've lost
and shadowing their strange ambivalence
about the very things they claim to love —
slim-waisted, self-absorbed, possessed by a greed
for something they can't name, their only claim
on our attention their attractiveness,
they smile at one another in the end,
hemmed in by the plots of an older pair
who seem to share a passionless marriage,
then dance upon a balcony whose rail
swirls into an outpouring of arc-lit stars.
　　　　　Earlier, in a night scene, the camera cuts
to the slow-rolling New York ferry, and shows,
over the wash of the union violins,
the city, both in and flying past the frame,
as it was seen by no one at the time —
echoing; dark; the deep, unmetered roar
of the traffic breaking over the waves;
it seems for this one moment that
the real life of the boroughs might break through
delivering the strangeness of those lives,
as if we were the angels, newly sent,
who, standing on a tenement's warped stairs,
shuddered at the blur of circumstance
while tasting the boarders' palpable fear —
city of people sitting in dyed woolens
before cabinet-sized radios;
city of Marxist pamphleteers, and bosses

skimming the profits from the market stalls;
the red blush of the apples in the ricks
and blue tint of the fish laid out on ice
are now forever lost, though the low sound
of that one night, captured by accident
in a confetti musical, broadcasts
your presence like a clear tone on a dial.
        And this is how I've come to know the world,
through images in which my conscience
wanders like a beam, yet, never spent,
inhabits too the dusty screening rooms—
in *Shall We Dance*, Astaire, as Pete Peters,
dances at the end with a line of chorus girls
who each wear a Ginger Rogers mask,
the real Ginger, of course, hiding among them—
and maybe this is what I know about love,
the bemused wonderment and joy as each
dons and then takes off the pasteboard mask and curls,
until, smiling in the center ring, the real
Ginger sweeps affectedly into his arms,
with just the fraying at the edge, and the blue
spot that hovers briefly near her eyes
to show how studious their labor was
late one Thursday afternoon on the set,
when the bored crew eating lunch off to the side
became the first to notice how the trained arc lights
allowed the couple to recede, until
the windmill motions of their arms and legs
outran their passion by a mere half-beat;
but whether it was passion for each other,
fame, or something else at one remove
the film itself can't say, commemorating
as it does just the blight of vanished rooms.

Pornography

Those women who remove their clothing piece
by piece; who linger over the lingerie;
pout as they finger nipple and clit; release
themselves with cries flung like bits of potter's clay;

who notices when their abandon dies
into a narrow margin, chafed and raw;
the poverty within their luxuries
apparent in the clenched fist, dull eyes, locked jaw —

who sees that freedom is in fact a jail
made up of dioramas and arcades
in which they shudder, handcuffed to a rail
for all the connoisseurs of these old trades;

who scoffs at the weight of guilt, yet mines its poise;
who mourns the partial handling of these joys?

Stewart Granger

Stewart Granger, when he died,
was famous, if obscure,
for having worn a Scottish plaid
when still a prisoner,

and what the papers said of him
was that he'd disapproved
of the many films on whose bright scrim
he'd chased, and fought, and loved.

That disapproval, though hard won,
was taken as a fault;
the grumbling of a sour old man
over the bread and salt.

His disaffection with his work
had one cause he would own;
after he left his regiment
they were killed to a man

in the bright sun of North Africa —
so, while he filled the screens
in drive-ins across America,
and girls bought magazines

to keep him by their beds at night,
his lone survivor's guilt
made him scoff at the trade of light,
no matter how well skilled.

Stewart Granger, when he died,
made us consider him
not as the man with a young bride
who posed on a high beam,

but as a soiled practitioner
of another, more desperate art;
keeping one's faith as the curtains stir
and daylight leaves the yard.

Gambier

A thought about *my* place in the long war
the intellectuals and poets fought
to a standstill in 1944;

the shooting war continuing full force,
life as we all know it half on hold;
gas, sugar, eggs, and butter scarce,

wardens pacing the alleyways at night
checking for escaping light, their cards
showing the blue silhouettes of airplanes;

who had to bear the possibility
of dying in the street, and at all costs avoid
being seen against the grey wash of the Thames.

Against this backdrop the new critics fought
for subjects not respected up till then;
one sees it in their pictures, the tense nights

spent poring over Tennyson or Donne,
mayflies buzzing at the copper lamp,
the pocked moon shining over a field

in Iowa, Ohio, Michigan.
And if indeed they won, what was the yield;
a way of living deep within the line?

When I look at one old picture, taken
in Gambier one summer night, my only thought
is God, that Nancy Tate was beautiful;

if I'd been there, I surely would have been
flirting over the potato salad,
knowing yet again that I'd confused

the beautiful with something like success,
yet unable to stop; my awkwardness
my only contribution to the night.

And there, in the dusk beneath the catalpa,
Berryman looking sly, Lowell assured,
while Tate recites the catalog of ships.

The Scale of Light

Drawn by what he wants to implicate
in the resistance of the bourgeoisie,
the scholar, sitting on a harp-shaped chair
while the projector shudders with banked light,
picks out a detail on the plaster screen,
flips the shutter, and gazes once more at
Hitler's procession through Montparnasse,
the cameramen and staff elated as
the motorcade sweeps past the boarded doors—
and there, within a yard
crowded with trip wire, burnt hoops, and drums,
the white flags of surrender have been dyed
the color of the banished government;
the purpose simple, obscenely so, within
the backstreet kitchen gardens of the slums—
here the film flutters, and the auditor
strains forward toward the cone of dirty light—
far back, behind an open outhouse door,
a child has pulled a rifle from a sack;
one of many such Resistance men
chosen for the unlikelihood
of their involvement with the underground;
and, looking backward, slips behind a fence
to gather from the air
the rifle's sharp report among the whistling
tiles and cisterns of a vacant bottling works.
The speeding of the motorcade beneath
the angels on the deep porches of the arch
is still somehow at odds
with the bright chill of that long-shadowed day,
as if the chromes and red insignia were bit
by acid in an otherwise faultlessly rolling screen.
The scholar, drawn by inclination, love,
and the necessities of his career,

has studied for some years
the media's creation of the war,
the instantaneous transmission of whose scenes
made terror commonplace
to millions in their homes; but a new sort
of terror; nickel-plated as it were
by the harsh irreality of the news,
that, crackling over the speakers in a voice
from heaven or the depots of Lorraine,
left the listeners soul-divided and unsure
amid the covered furniture and stoves.
It is the scholar's thesis that this world,
refracted as it was by plate and film,
gave birth, through stagings, acts, and newsreels, to
a second, mediated world of glass:
young idols posing in exotic dress
before a riot of grey dunes or waves;
brush-animated characters engrossed
by complicated labors of revenge,
the small-time metaphysics of their plots
reflected in the Xs of their eyes.
According to the scholar, this new world
grew heartless as the first, as it advanced
and labored in the space
it opened, desolate or not, to all.
Some years before the documentary
the West unknowingly mixed tragedy
and its lurid awareness of the same
when the Hindenburg suddenly burst into flame,
the edges of the canvas indistinct
through the fringe and kyrie of heated gas;
the skeleton frame, moored still to the ground
by a long chain arcing upward to a cloud,
an incandescent hive of wind-buffeted fire—
and as a panicked voice called out the end
and the wind gusting past the microphone
took on the private resonance of dread,

a photographer bent to his camera and took
an image that was seen throughout the world
as the craft, disintegrating, fell to rest
among the weeds and oil drums of Bayonne.

His pageantry already tarnished by
the unknown slaughter in the Berlin slums,
the führer will soon step down from his car
and, whether due to his elation at the arch
or a hitch in the film rolling close by,
will dance that herky-jerky step, his cap
of field lieutenant's blue low on his brow;
and soon the world will once again relearn
how dangerous a simple joy can be
as it takes in the image of this man
alone amidst his generals; head bowed
in thought above Napoleon's dark tomb.

Kehoutek

Late in the evening, the newscast done
and the heat still rising in the room,
I put away my thoughts again
and, shrugging on my coat, left home;
then saw that pale, unsteady broom

sweeping above the alleyway,
a glut of pearl the wind had stalked.
Brightening against the day,
it had shone when the ancients walked
their battlements, and from it, chalked

the planets from the stars, then rolled
the sky in one leaved hemisphere.
Now, shining dully as worked gold,
the comet traced the earth's career
through empty space, with glittering hair.

So I set out in my rough coat
to follow through the neighborhood
the trail of that unsteady mote
as it guttered in solitude,
and ended where some others stood

on the lakefront promenade,
the benches empty in the dark.
As I walked up, the trail was laid
with a blue profusion of spark,
the sun's wind cutting through its arc.

I met an old professor, who
in a long coat and patterned vest,
took notes until we lost the view
behind the black posts in the west,
then joined me as I turned and crossed

the broad lawns toward the neighborhood.
His discipline aside, my lack
of one no barrier, we stood
at night's end with Gary at our backs,
that rough spark blowing in the stacks.

As we'd strolled the lakefront walk,
he told me how he'd seen
the star before he learned to talk,
when both his parents still had been
my age. Soon afterward the lien

was closed on their first property,
and he was sent to a relative.
The star to him was a memory,
and with its incandescent staff
returned, if not their time, their love.

Later, I saw in my mind's eye
his life's career: success at school
and at the university;
first books; and in his mind that cruel
separation, and its unstable rule.

If love's first presence in the mind
is like the faint blue trace of one
who, figured on a widemouthed bowl,
is, when the bowl is tilted, gone;
then love is never really done;

the slightest impetus toward change
recovering an opposite
whose sensuality, though strange,
demands assent and threatens drought
in a harp strung from the wastes of light.

Rolling like a pearl in ink,
the comet draws its halo from
the glut through which the planets sink,
scattering ice chips from its plume
like trinkets from a raided tomb.

That star returned, we know the past
wrinkling in its plume of jet—
however much we know, a vast
emptiness gusts in its trail; and yet,
the tumbling comet says, and yet.

New England Winter

1

The pollard elm's stark eyes of wood,
paled by the long drought,
darken, as though a flow of blood
ran from crown to root,

while a pigeon huddled on a branch
leaps in its cantering flight,
its blurred wings, through the avalanche
of snow, a tinted white.

The sun, on these abstracted days,
opens a shapeless sack
of frostscraps and glitter, ice chips and haze,
to spill on its widening track

and haunts the living corridor of trees
until perspective turns
the black stumps into mounds of ice
that breathe like covered urns.

2

Here, the room's interior
softly creaks and pops,
the wind pressing against the door
while my ambition drops.

The dust, with guarded discipline,
has jeweled the clock's knit gears,
and, when its whim is ravening,
turns the hours into years.

I spoke of ghosts too lightly once,
but meant no more by it
than a rattling of skeletons
that strengthens to regret;

now, pale as the imagined space
between the clock's two hands,
their lives again take weight and trace
through appetite's demands.

3

Today I woke and found myself
within the crackling marge
of a sickness that announced itself
like a wind in the deep gorge

and, as I struggled, I let go
my rage, and dreams, and love;
and for that instant, finally saw
how little I'd dreamed of.

So, waking early to my work
in the selfless light of dawn,
I saw the ocean's battered mark
on twig, eave, and stone;

and heard a voice within a room
where none was before;
white as the ocean the dust on the broom;
rough blossoms on the floor.

Acknowledgments

Grateful acknowledgment is made to the editors of the following publications in which the poems below first appeared.

Thomas Sayers Ellis, *The Good Junk*

A Gathering of the Tribes: "Barbershop"
AGNI: "A Baptist Beat," "Barracuda," "Sticks," "The Roll Call"
Callaloo: "Fatal April," "On Display," "Shooting Back," "Tambourine Tommy," "The Market"
Hambone: "Giant Steps," "Take Me Out to the Go-Go"
Harvard Review: "Tambourine"
The Kenyon Review: "Cowbell," "Tapes," "The Moonlite Inn"
Ploughshares: "Being There"
The Southern Review: "View of the Library of Congress from Paul Laurence Dunbar High School"
UWEZO: "Block Party," "Faggot," "Stayed Back"

"The Break of Dawn" and "On Display" appeared in *In the Tradition: An Anthology of Young Black Writers,* Eds. Kevin Powell and Ras Baraka, Harlem River Press, 1992.
"A Baptist Beat," "Shooting Back," "Sticks," and "View of the Library of Congress from Paul Laurence Dunbar High School" appeared in *The Garden Thrives: Twentieth Century African American Poetry,* Ed. Clarence Major, HarperCollins, 1996.
"A Baptist Beat" also appeared in *Between God and Gangsta Rap: Bearing Witness to Black Culture,* Michael Eric Dyson, Oxford University Press, 1995.

A special thanks to Mrs. Jeanette Ellis, Askold Melnyczuk, Seamus Heaney, Lucie Brock-Broido, Michael S. Harper, Charles H. Rowell, Doris Craig, Cynthia Jones, and The Dark Room Collective (especially Sharan Strange, Kevin Young, Nehassaiu de Gannes, John Keene, Tracy K. Smith, and Major Jackson), Kelly Sloane, and the MacDowell Colony for residencies that gave me the time and space to complete this collection.

Larissa Szporluk, *Prowler's Universe*

AGNI: "Ideogram," "Ghost Continent"
The Berkeley Poetry Review: "Gemini"
Colorado Review: "Anhedonia"
Englynion: "Benefits of Drowning"
Harvard Review: "Allegro of the Earth," "Envoy of the Boat"
Hayden's Ferry Review: "Mauvaises Terres"
Heartbeat: "Price of Ruin"
Indiana Review: "Krell," "Bluebells," "Round Face in a Little Town,"
    "Koan," "Solar Wind," "Radiolaria," "Ignis Fatuus"
Iris: "Avalanche"
Lullwater Review: "Libido," "Age of Piracy"
Northeast Journal: "Quiet Emergency"
Northwest Review: "Prowler's Universe"
Poem: "A Capella"
Poet Lore: "Agnosia," "Swordfish Season"
The Santa Clara Review: "Devolution"
The Santa Monica Review: "Under the Bridge," "The Bystander's Power"

Special thanks to Macklin Smith, Alice Fulton, Rita Dove, Greg Orr,
and Charles Wright for their insight and assistance.

Joe Osterhaus, *The Domed Road*

AGNI: "Sweet Decision" and "The Scale of Light"
Antioch Review: "Pepper"
The Formalist: "Kehoutek"
The Journal: "To an Aborted Child," "Husk" (under the title "The Summer
    Storms"), and "Shall We Dance" (as part of a longer poem titled "Two
    on Film")
The Nebraska Review: "New England Winter"

This book was designed by Will Powers. It is set in Charlotte and Franklin Gothic type by Stanton Publication Services, Inc. and manufactured by BookCrafters on acid-free paper.

Cover design by Jeanne Lee.